RUNNING RECORDS

Running Records: A Self-Tutoring Guide

PETER H. JOHNSTON

State University of New York at Albany

STENHOUSE PUBLISHERS

York, Maine

Stenhouse Publishers, P.O. Box 360, York, Maine 03909

www.stenhouse.com

Copyright © 2000 by Peter H. Johnston

CREDITS ARE ON PAGE 53

ISBN 1-57110-321-X

Interior design by Geri Davis, The Davis Group
Typeset by Technologies 'N Typography
Manufactured in the United States of America on acid-free paper
21 20 19 18   16 15 14 13

To Dame Marie M. Clay

I dedicate this book to Dame Marie M. Clay as a token of my gratitude and respect. Marie provided the inspiration and the conceptual underpinnings for much of what I know about children's literate development. Of course that does not distinguish me from a very large group of people. My debt goes beyond that. In the original book, *Knowing Literacy*, Marie had joint authorship of these chapters because the concept and development of running records was hers and because her careful and insightful responses had been part of the development of those chapters. With her usual generosity, she suggested that with this version it should be viewed as my work.

CONTENTS

Introduction   ix

PART ONE
Recording Oral Reading   1

PART TWO
Interpreting Oral Reading Records   21

APPENDIXES

A
Sheet for Running Record Analysis   41

B
Practice Running Records   42

References   51

INTRODUCTION

This book is intended to teach you how to take running records of children's oral reading, to make sense of them, and to use them to focus your teaching. Running records were first published in New Zealand. They were developed for a longitudinal research study of children's literacy learning in the first year of school (Clay 1966, 1972). Using a research approach adapted from the field of developmental psychology they provide a way of observing how children work on problem-solving a complex task. They are, without doubt, the single most useful technique for documenting early reading processes. Having said that, however, I must point out that the recording system itself is only useful in the hands of an informed teacher. Learning how to take running records is not simply a matter of learning a shorthand for recording children's oral reading errors. It involves learning a way of thinking about reading and its acquisition. I have woven some of this into the two parts of this book, but a more thorough treatment can be found in the book from which these chapters have been taken entitled *Knowing Literacy: Constructive Literacy Assessment*. Other works you might consult include Marie Clay's *Becoming Literate* (1991) or her *Observation Survey of Early Literacy Achievement* (1993a) and *Reading Recovery: A Guidebook for Teachers in Training* (1993b), or Irene Fountas and Gay Su Pinnell's *Guided Reading: Good First Teaching for All Children* (1996).

$\mathcal{R}$ECORDING ORAL READING

$\mathcal{M}$ature reading is generally done silently in the privacy of one's own head. This is not a problem for self-evaluation, but it poses a bit of a problem for teachers who wish to assess their students' reading. Fortunately, beginning readers tend to read aloud quite naturally, even when asked to read silently. Oral reading has been used for many years to assess the kind of language processes taking place in the head of the reader. This assessment can be only an estimate of the reader's mental processes, however. Oral reading and silent reading are not the same thing (Leu 1982; Schumm and Baldwin 1989). The two serve quite different functions for adults. Nonetheless, there is sufficient similarity between the two to make analyzing students' oral reading a useful way to understand the way they process language when they read.

Over the years, oral reading has occasionally suffered some bad press because it is not really the same as mature reading (Allington 1983). In addition, oral reading as a classroom round-robin activity can be a socially threatening situation for readers who struggle with word recognition. Oral reading is most appropriate in choral or shared reading, or in the context of readers' theater, in which prepared reading can be done as a public performance. However, for purposes of evaluation, oral reading need not be stressful or done so frequently as to suggest that it is the most important or only form of reading.

Running records of oral reading are basically a vehicle for error analysis—the imaginative challenge of figuring out the logic of error. Like oral reading, errors have had a bad rap. For teachers, the most useful aspect of errors is that people do not make them randomly. There is always a reason for them. If you can figure out the reason, then you know where to best use your instructional expertise and how to avoid confusing the student.

Detailed analysis of oral reading errors began seriously with the work of Ken Goodman (Goodman 1965; Goodman, Watson, and Burke 1987) and Rose-Marie Weber (1970), both of whom used the term *miscue* rather than *error*. Analysis of oral reading is a particular example of error analysis (hence my use of "error"). Because errors are not made randomly, and because each is partly right, they suggest the kind of mental processing taking place and allow us to examine the leading edge of a learner's development. An individual error is less informative than a pattern of errors, and the clearer the pattern, the more helpful it is for informing teaching.

Ways to Record Oral Reading

An experienced teacher in the early elementary grades can often listen to a reader and get a good idea of the strategies being used and the reader's state of development. However, generally it is not enough simply to listen to oral reading and depend on your memory. Memories are frail and are not much use to present to anyone as a sole source of information. You could tape-record a child's reading; this is useful and certainly has the advantage of fidelity, but in the long run it is inconvenient: you don't have immediate access to a particular reading and you can't focus on the important aspects without listening to the whole thing. It is much better to have a graphic record of the oral reading so you can get the instructionally relevant information at a glance, compare earlier and later perform-ance, and keep the record conveniently filed and accessible.

Many people have devised ways to record oral reading errors; each has its advantages and disadvantages. In this chapter, with the help of Marie Clay, I describe how to record children's oral reading using *running records,* a method she devised and presented in her book *An Observation Survey of Early Literacy Achieve-ment* (Clay 1993a), to which you should refer. (I have taught classes using this book and its earlier editions for the past sixteen years and have yet to encounter a secondhand copy). To use the method, you simply take a blank (or lined) piece of paper or a special record sheet, and use shorthand to write down the child's read-ing behaviors as he or she reads aloud. An overview of Clay's shorthand recording scheme is presented in Table 1. There are other methods of recording, including the commonly used Informal Reading Inventories (IRIs), which I refer to later in the chapter. However, in order to avoid confusion for those who are already familiar with IRIs, I should note that running records are different from IRIs in one important way. To take a running record, you do not need to have a copy of the text to write on; you just need a piece of paper. This makes running records more difficult to learn than informal reading inventory procedures, but it is also a major advantage. It allows you to record oral reading at any time, from any book, without any preparation such as photocopying or dittoing the pages or having extra copies of the book available. This makes the recording system very flexible.

Running records have other advantages too. First, because you don't have to do anything except pick up a pen and paper when a child is reading, you are more likely to actually make them. Second, running records do not establish a "test" environment (although whether the child feels it is a test depends on many factors,

TABLE 1

Recording Symbols for Running Records

General format:	Child's response	Final response
	Word in the text	Teacher prompt

WHAT IS SAID	DURING READING	AFTER READING
Correct response	✓	✓
Omission	—	—
		text word
Substitution	spoken word	spoken word
		text word
Insertion	spoken word	spoken word
		—
Repetition[1]	R	R
Attempt	attempt | attempt	attempt | attempt
		text word
Appeal for help	APP	attempt | APP
		text word
Teacher prompt:		
tells the word	‾‾‾ |‾ T	— |‾
		text word | T
asks to try section again[2]	| TA	| TA

1. Number of repetitions is recorded with a superscript. Size of repetition is recorded with a line from the R to the beginning of the repeated section.
2. The line extends vertically from the beginning to the end of the section to be repeated with TA (for "try again") alongside it.

including the child's experiences in the past, the relationship with the person taking the record, and the situation in which the reading is done). Running records can be done frequently on whatever the child happens to be reading. Third, unlike IRIs, which often use texts assumed to be comparable to the level of the basal reader on which the child will ultimately be placed, running records use a variety of children's books taken from the classroom or chosen by the student.

Using the Tape and the Text

The rest of this chapter will show you how to record oral reading errors; the next chapter will help you figure out what they might mean. Each kind of error a beginning reader might make is illustrated in the examples on the tape that accompanies this book. (My use of the audiotape is modeled on the superb Early Reading Inservice Course [ERIC] developed by the New Zealand Department of

Education, which also developed the record-keeping system in greater detail.) The number of each example is announced on the tape. Use a blank piece of paper to make a record of each example. After listening to each example, stop the tape and return to this text to check your record against the one provided here.

Learning now to make running records takes time. The critical ingredient is practice. You wouldn't expect to learn shorthand overnight, so don't expect to learn running records overnight. Your facility will improve with practice. Fortunately, you can easily practice on the sly, and no one is likely to be looking over your shoulder. If you are a teacher practicing running records with your students, you will find your students will be very understanding about your clumsiness. Always explain to them what you are doing at the outset; tell them they can look at the record afterward and you will explain it to them. This makes the process less threatening for the students and a learning experience for all concerned.

Often people learning to record oral reading tape-record the reading so that they can stop the tape to make time for writing, or go back to make sure they got everything right. This tends to make you dependent on the tape recorder, and using a tape recorder makes running records (or IRIs) take at least twice the time they would otherwise. As a result, there is a good chance that you will do fewer of them and eventually none at all. Occasionally using recordings for self-checking and for repeated record-taking in order to build fluency (like repeated readings) can help. However, it becomes a hindrance if you continually stop and start the tape to try to keep up. Patience and practice are what you should rely on.

Beginning the Record

At the top of the page always note the reader's name, the date, the book and page(s) being read, and any special conditions, such as whether or how often the book has been read previously or whether the book has been read to the child.

Words Read Correctly

Each word read correctly is represented by a check mark (✓). Thus the following rendition of a text by a child would be recorded as shown:

TEXT:	Today the class went to the zoo.
	We saw an elephant and a monkey.
READER:	Today the class went to the zoo.
	We saw an elephant and a monkey.
RUNNING RECORD:	✓ ✓ ✓ ✓ ✓ ✓ ✓ ✓
	✓ ✓ ✓ ✓ ✓ ✓ ✓ ✓

Note that there is one check mark for each word, and that they are arranged in exactly the way the words are arranged on the page so that we can tell which check represents which word. Now you try it with Example 1 on the tape. The correct record is shown alongside the text below.

"Go home,"   ✓ ✓

said the hens.   ✓ ✓ ✓

"No," said Little Pig.   ✓ ✓ ✓ ✓

"Go home,"   ✓ ✓

said the ducks.   ✓ ✓ ✓

"No," said Little Pig.   ✓ ✓ ✓ ✓

"Go home,"   ✓ ✓

said the cows.   ✓ ✓ ✓

"No," said Little Pig.   ✓ ✓ ✓ ✓

"Go home,"   ✓ ✓

said the sheep.   ✓ ✓ ✓

"No," said Little Pig.   ✓ ✓ ✓ ✓

"Go home,"   ✓ ✓

said the butcher,   ✓ ✓ ✓

"or I'll make you into   ✓ ✓ ✓ ✓ ✓

sausages."   ✓

"Yes, I will,"   ✓ ✓ ✓

said Little Pig.   ✓ ✓ ✓

Words Omitted

Sometimes, deliberately or accidentally, readers skip over a word. We record this with a dash (—). After we have finished the running record we go back and write the omitted word beneath the dash, separating the two with a horizontal line. This is the standard practice for making the record. Record the reader's behavior and, after the record is complete, return to add the relevant words underneath each recorded deviation from the text. A running record with omissions should be recorded as shown below:

TEXT: There was once a jolly farmer
who had a red tractor.

READER: There was a jolly farmer   ✓ ✓ — ✓ ✓ ✓
had a red tractor.   — ✓ ✓ ✓ ✓

      ✓ ✓ $\dfrac{-}{once}$ ✓ ✓ ✓

      $\dfrac{-}{who}$ ✓ ✓ ✓ ✓

Your record of this done while the student was reading would look like the record alongside the student transcript above. After the child finished reading you would add the details from the text so that your record would look like the one below the first.

Now try to record the second example on the tape. The text for it is:

TAPE EXAMPLE 2

> "I'm looking for a house,"
> said the little brown mouse.

Your first pass at the running record should look something like this:

✓   ✓   ✓   ✓   ✓

✓   –   ✓   ✓   ✓

After you have finished taking the running record, add to it the details—the word omitted and a line separating the two. It should look something like this:

✓   ✓   ✓   ✓   ✓

✓ $\frac{-}{the}$ ✓   ✓   ✓

When you are learning to take running records it is very important to wait until the end to add the actual word missed. It only takes a minute to add these finishing touches to the running record. If you try to do it during the reading, you will miss a lot of other details of the reading. When you become fluent, you may be able to add some of these finishing touches on the run, but you will find it a lot easier to learn the method if you do it in two steps to begin with.

Words Substituted

Younger readers commonly substitute a different word for the one on the page. When this happens, simply write down the word the reader says, and later fill in the word that was in the text. For example:

TEXT:	Harry was a good boy.	
READER:	Harry was a nice boy.	✓ ✓ ✓ $\frac{nice}{good}$ ✓

Now try your hand at recording the example on the tape. The text being read is the following:

TAPE EXAMPLE 3:   *The Dragon's Birthday* by Margaret Mahy (1984a)

> At the same time, Richard
> and Claire, Henry and Huia and Billy,

were going up the road wearing
their dragon costume.

Your running record for this should look something like this:

✓ ✓ ✓ ✓ ✓
✓ ✓ $\frac{Harry}{Henry}$ ✓ ✓ ✓ ✓
✓ $\frac{coming}{going}$ ✓ ✓ ✓ ✓
✓ ✓ ✓

Notice that although two words are substituted, the meaning has not been lost, and the substitutions reflect some of the print features of the author's words. The reader is striving to make sense *and* to match what he says with what he sees.

Words Inserted

Sometimes children add words to the reading that are not in the text. To record this, simply write the words into the record just as you record substitutions. Later, add a dash *underneath* the added word to indicate that there was no matching word in the text. An example of an insertion would look like this:

TEXT: I went to the shops.
READER: I went down to the shops.   ✓ ✓ $\underline{down}$ ✓ ✓ ✓

Now take your turn at this recording with the example on the tape.

TAPE EXAMPLE 4: *Old Tuatara* by Joy Cowley (1984)

Old Tuatara sat in the sun.
He sat and sat and sat.
"Asleep," said the fantail.
"Asleep," said the gull.
"Asleep," said the frog.
"Asleep," said the fly.
"Not asleep," said Old Tuatara.

Each of the animals thinks Old Tuatara (an ancient and almost extinct reptile) is asleep, but the hapless fly finds out he is not). Note the relish with which Samantha reads this passage (even though it has been read to her and by her a number of times before). This book is an excellent example of what a good author can do with a handful of words and a good illustrator. You probably also noticed how easily Sam picked up on a connection to another book, *Fantail, Fantail* (Mahy 1984b), which also ends with the fly being devoured. She actually quotes the final words from the book ("Goodbye, fly"). Would it make sense to ask Sam questions to see whether she understands *Old Tuatara?* I don't think so. Your running record for this fourth tape example should look like this:

I thought Sam's connection to another book (the next example on the tape) was important enough to note on the record.

Sometimes recording substitutions is not as simple as you might at first think. Remember, the idea is to record deviations from the text, word by word. Try the following example.

TAPE EXAMPLE 5:   *Fantail, Fantail* by Margaret Mahy (1984b)

"Fantail, Fantail,
have some cheese."
"No. No. No.
I don't like cheese."
"Fantail, Fantail,
have some peas."
"No. No. No.
I don't like peas."
"Fantail, Fantail,
have some pie."
"No. No. No.
I don't like pie."

Here is the running record for this reading:

```
✓ ✓
✓ ✓ ✓
✓ ✓ ✓
✓  do   not  ✓ ✓
  don't   -
✓ ✓
✓ ✓ ✓
✓ ✓ ✓
✓  do   not  ✓ ✓
  don't   -
✓ ✓
✓ ✓ ✓
✓ ✓ ✓
✓  do   not  ✓ ✓
  don't   -
```

The interesting and positive thing about Emily's reading error is that she substitutes book language for the more natural language actually in the text: books are more likely to avoid contractions, using, for example, "do not" rather than "don't." The down side is that she is not as concerned about matching one spoken word to one printed word.

Self-Corrections

When we make an error in our reading, often (though not always) we stop to correct it. This is a very important behavior because it is usually evidence that we are cross-checking one set of cues with another. Every time readers do this they learn something. Self-corrections are recorded by using the letters *SC*, as in the following example:

TEXT:	Once upon a time there
	lived a dragon.
SUSAN:	Once upon a time there	✓ ✓ ✓ ✓ ✓
	was [pause] lived a dragon.	was/sc ✓ ✓
		lived

Susan may have used her knowledge of sentence structure (syntax) and perhaps of other stories to predict that *was* would follow *there*. However, when her eyes reached the actual word she did not see the letters that fit with her prediction. Instead of the letters *w-a-s* she saw the letters *l-i-v-e-d*. In light of this new information, she corrected herself. *This is an indication of healthy reading.* Susan was being efficient in trying to predict what was coming, but she also showed a concern for accurate representation of the text. We call this "self-correcting from print" because the print leads to the self-correction. This interpretation of Susan's mental processes is plausible because her first effort made sense and it fit the structure of the sentence; the only mismatch was with the print. The next example on the tape illustrates this type of self-correction. The following is the text:

TAPE EXAMPLE 6:   *Who Took the Farmer's Hat?* by Joan Nodset (1989)

> He saw Squirrel.
> "Squirrel, did you see
> my old brown hat?"

The running record for this would look like this:

Self-corrections do not always occur this way. Sometimes incongruities in meaning prompt the correction. Consider the following:

> The girl's hair was really quite ornate. Her bows for the audience were
> received with much applause.

In this passage, you probably read the word *bows* incorrectly and then returned to correct it. You made a plausible reading but discovered later in the sentence that it did not make sense. This is called "self-correcting from meaning." Good readers engage in both types of self-correction as needed, showing their awareness that reading requires a balanced use of the available cues.

Recording self-corrections is the point at which most disagreement will occur among different recorders. Remember that in order to record something as a self-correction we must infer a mental activity that we cannot see, so we rely on little clues like voice inflection to help us. We have to decide whether the reader was just figuring out a word or actually making an error and then going back and correcting it. Such situations occur often enough with self-corrections that they do require some caution in interpretation. We will get more practice at this along the way.

There are also other things that make self-corrections difficult to interpret. First, not all self-corrections are made out loud. As readers mature, they become increasingly able to correct their errors silently. Second, some older readers become overly concerned about relatively trivial errors, such as substituting *a* for *the*. Although this kind of error might be an important place for beginning readers to learn, in a more mature reader it might be too much of a good thing, slowing the reader unnecessarily and diverting attention from the bigger picture.

Repetitions

Sometimes readers, having read a word, a sentence, or some other segment of text, decide to go back and reread it. There are numerous reasons for this. They might reread because what they read the first time did not seem to make sense, or they might reread to savor what the writer said or to help figure out a difficult word, or they might reread to get a better flow if there were several difficult words in the sentence. Repetitions are recorded with the letter R and a line, as in the following example:

TEXT: The spider grabbed the fly
and wrapped it up.

READER: The spider grabbed grabbed the fly
the spider grabbed the fly
and wrapped wrapped wrapped it up.

As shown in this example, a numerical superscript is used to indicate more than one repetition. Also, notice how the notation is used for either a single word or larger sections of text. The repetition of a larger section is indicated by drawing a line from the R back to the beginning of the repeated segment.

Try recording repetitions from the following text.

TAPE EXAMPLE 7: *My Bike* by Craig Martin (1982)

On Tuesday I rode my bike
around the tree,
over the bridge,
under the branches
and through the puddle.

The running record should resemble this one:

Now try the next example:

TAPE EXAMPLE 8: *Saturday Morning* by Lesley Moyes (1983)

"Dad, the car is clean,
and so are we," said Mark.

Here's how the running record should look:

Problem-Solving

Often when a reader does not recognize a word right away, he will try to figure it out, possibly making several attempts. These attempts are frequently made out loud, especially by younger readers. Each attempt should be recorded, because they tell us a lot about the reader's strategies for figuring out words. Consider the examples of readers reading the following sentence.

TEXT: She could see people swimming in the water.
READER 1: She could see people s/sw/swim/swimming in the water.
READER 2: She could see people sing in the water—swimming in the water.
READER 3: She could see people swing/ing/swim/swimming in the water.
READER 4: She could see people—in the water—swimming in the water.

Each reader was successful in figuring out the unknown word, and each tackled the word in a different manner. Even a single example of problem-solving gives us some useful information, but a pattern of several examples gives us more dependable information.

Students' problem-solving on words is recorded using vertical rules, as shown below:

TEXT: We all went to the fair.
READER: We all went to the f/fire/far/fair.   ✓ ✓ ✓ ✓ ✓ f|fire|far|✓
                                                                      fair

Try your hand at recording problem-solving using the next taped example.

TAPE EXAMPLE 9: *The Dragon's Birthday* by Margaret Mahy (1984a)

The next morning, a boy named Richard
said to his sister Claire,

"Today's the dragon's birthday."

"Everyone knows that," said Claire.

"Poor dragon. No one is brave enough
to go up to his cave and say,
'Happy birthday.'"

"Perhaps we could go," said Richard.

"It's too dangerous," said their mother.

"He might frizzle you up."

Your running record should resemble this one:

Recording problem-solving is not easy. In fact, it may be the hardest part of taking running records. However, the information that it provides about the strategies the reader used to figure out unfamiliar words is very important and well worth the effort. You will notice in the reading in Tape Example 9 that Nick was very consistent in his attempts to figure out the words. One part of your record may have been different from mine. I recorded Nick's figuring out of the word *brave* as a self-correction rather than as a word that he finally figured out: I wrote "SC" at the end instead of a check mark. I interpreted his intonation on "braf" as an indication that he was satisfied that he had made a word. His voice had an air of finality about it. But then, having said it, he changed his mind. It sounded to me as though it was a self-correction. You may differ. Our difference on the matter is not particularly important unless we have hardly any other examples of Nick's reading. If this were the only example of self-correction and it was doubtful, we might seek some more data. Multiple examples are important for establishing patterns.

Sometimes rather than sounding out words, readers will spell them. This is recorded with capital letters instead of lowercase ones.

Sometimes we witness very complex strategies for figuring out words, and great persistence in doing so. Listen to the next example on the tape, in which Nick figures out the word *midnight*.

TAPE EXAMPLE 10

for his midnight swim.

The running record for this reading looks like this:

Readings as complicated as this one may outfox you in the beginning, but you can simply make a side note later of some of the strategies that you heard. In this example, Nick first tried to figure the word out left to right, then he backed out to get the context and have another go, then he recognized a word he knew within the word, which finally allowed the whole thing to come together. I recorded the outcome as a self-correction rather than as simply correctly figured out because he said "midingth" with a tone of "Got it!" and then returned to a puzzling-out tone before finally reading the phrase correctly.

Time to Take Stock

If you normally write in small print, you might have found yourself cramped for space when the reader repeated a section and corrected an earlier error. You will probably find it easier if you allow yourself to be a little more expansive in your recording. The next example on the tape should help you begin to get the feel of putting together what you have learned so far. Nick is reading.

TAPE EXAMPLE 11: *Busy Beavers* by M. Barbara Brownell (1988)

Page 2:
Beside a pond, a beaver snacks on tall grass and weeds.
On land, beavers find trees to use for making their homes,
called lodges. They build the lodges in deep water.
A beaver swims back and forth from its home to the land.

Page 4:
This beaver is busy building
a dam to hold water back

in a pond. Soon the water will be
deep and will be a safe place
for the beaver to build its lodge.

With its sharp front teeth,
the beaver cuts a branch in two.
A hard orange coating on the
teeth keeps them from chipping
as the beaver bites through wood.

The running record should look something like this:

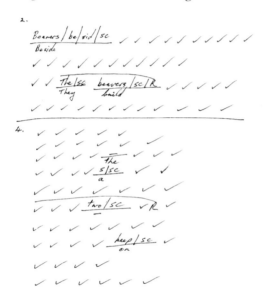

Notice how the page numbers are recorded at the left.

You might have found yourself at or beyond your limit in attempting to take this record. This should not be surprising. You are essentially in the process of learning shorthand and should not expect to become comfortable with it in only a few minutes. Fortunately, like reading, the more you do it, the easier it becomes. Indeed, you might like to rewind the tape and try Example 11 again. Just as beginning readers find rereading helpful for developing fluency, teachers beginning to take running records can develop fluency from repeating a record. Just be careful not to become addicted to tape recorders.

In recording Example 11, you might also have found that your running record was not the same as mine. Actually, there is more than one way to record this reading, depending on how you interpret certain reading behaviors. For example, Nick read one part as follows:

TEXT: Soon the water will be deep
              and will be a safe place . . .

NICK: Soon water will be deep
              and will be s—a safe place . . .

When I was making my record, I felt that Nick predicted the word *safe* and began to say it, but then encountered the actual word, *a*, noticed the discrepancy, and corrected his error. You might have interpreted it as suggesting that he skipped over *a* to *safe*, but then noticed the *a*. This would be recorded as follows:

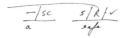

Again, some differences in interpretation are to be expected, but in the long run should not have serious consequences. One way to determine the correct interpretation is simply to ask the reader. For example, after he or she has finished reading you might ask, "How did you know to . . .?" or "I noticed that you . . . What were you thinking when you did that?" Provided these questions are not interpreted as calls to justify errors, you will often learn something about the reader's thinking. However, some children (and adults) are more able to recall their strategies than others.

One final reader behavior is worth recording. Sometimes readers realize they are stuck and ask for help. We record this with the letters *APP*, for "appeal." If the child attempts the word first, a record might look like this:

              p | panded | pandled | APP

In the next example on the tape Sam appeals to me for help, unnecessarily it turns out. You will have to listen carefully, as she whispers her appeal. Try to record it now.

TAPE EXAMPLE 12:   *Harry Goes to Funland* by Harriet Ziefert (1989)

              Harry even rode
              the roller coaster.

Your record should look like this:

Notice that I used a check mark at the end of the record because she finally figured the word out correctly. She did not make an error and then correct it, so it is not a self-correction.

An appeal to another person is a useful strategy for figuring things out and is important to note. However, if it occurs with any regularity on text that is not that difficult for the reader, it suggests a lack of independence and confidence. In such a case, teaching interactions should be examined to see what is producing the situation.

Sometimes children realize there is a problem, but neither appeal for help nor fix it themselves. In this case, I use a question mark to indicate the questioning inflection in the reader's voice.

Intervention

In general, when you are taking running records, you should intervene as little as possible because you are interested in learning how readers manage things themselves. However, occasionally there are times when it is appropriate to intervene, particularly when the usefulness of your subsequent records or your rapport with the reader is at risk. Sometimes children make a series of errors that compound themselves and stall their reading. When this happens, they either cease to read altogether or cease to read in a manner that is typical of their normal performance. The sensible thing for the teacher to do in this case is to help them get back on track and restart themselves by giving them a prompt to reread. Usually you would say, "Why don't you try that again?" and direct them to the beginning of the sentence, paragraph, page, or other meaning unit. This allows readers to approach the problematic section with greater momentum. It amounts to a prompted rereading. If they are successful at rectifying the problem, we have modeled a repair strategy (which we might later point out to them), and their subsequent reading tells us something about what they can do when given some strategic support.

However, interventions must be recorded so that they can be taken into account in our later interpretations. A prompted rereading can be recorded simply with the letters TA (try again), as in the following example:

TEXT: Once upon a time,
an old man planted
a little turnip.
He said to the little turnip,
"Grow, little turnip!"

BOB: Once upon a time,
an old man p/panded/pandled?
a little t/trip/trinip—turnip.
[Try that again.]
Once upon a time,
an old man p/planted
a little turnip.
He said to the little turnip,
"Grow, little turnip!"

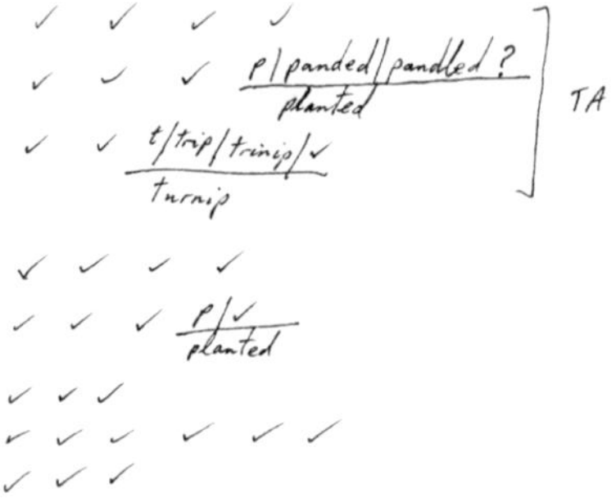

[Handwritten reading annotations with check marks appear to the right, including: "p/panded/pandled?" over "planted", "t/trip/trinip/✓" over "turnip", "p/✓" over "planted", bracketed and marked "TA"]

Notice that the whole repeated section is bracketed and marked "TA" for "try again." Basically this record tells you, "This section was not typical of Bob's reading, so I got him to take another run at it."

Try to record the next example on the tape. Sam is reading the text:

TAPE EXAMPLE 13: *I Can Read* by Margaret Malcolm (1983)

I read to my mother.
I read to my father.
I read to my nana.

Your record should look something like this:

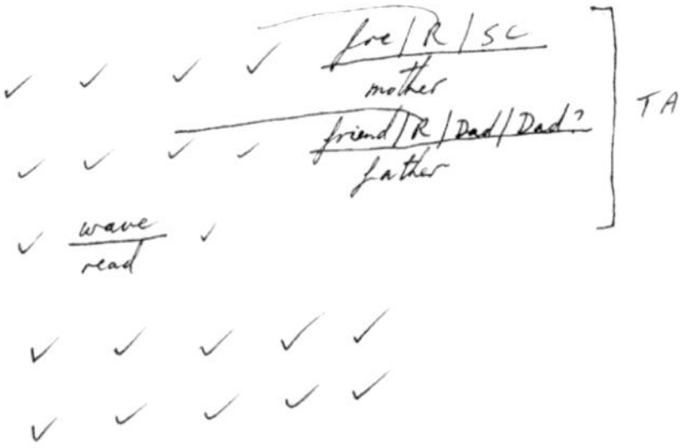

[Handwritten reading annotations with check marks, including: "fre/R/sc" over "mother", "friend/R/Dad/Dad?" over "father", "wave/read", bracketed and marked "TA"]

The reason Sam had trouble with this book is because she had just read the book *Going to School* (Cowley 1983a) and still had the melody of that book in her head. She noticed that the words and letters on the page did not match that melody, and her voice shows her confusion. Suddenly she realized exactly what had happened and she is able to read it the way it is supposed to be.

The second type of intervention you can make is actually telling the student the word. You should try to minimize the likelihood of having to do this—by introducing stories well (including any particularly awkward words) and by knowing the student well enough to predict how he or she will manage the book.

However, sometimes it is clear that introducing the context will give little or no support, or you know from your experience with the student that a particular word is out of her range. So you tell the child the word. When you do this, it is recorded by writing *T* in the bottom right corner of the record, as in the following example:

TEXT: We cannot go back to
        the old quarry.

READER: We cannot go back to   ✓ ✓ ✓ ✓ ✓
        the old [Teacher tells *quarry*].   ✓ ✓ —quarry— |T

Now try the next example on the tape.

TAPE EXAMPLE 14:   *Indian Two Feet and His Horse* by Margaret Friskey (1959)

He could sing.
He could dance.

Your record should look like this:

✓ ✓ ✓
✓ ✓ draw/d/d/drancee?/d
      dance   /T

Other Observations

Other types of reading behavior may be important for different children. For example, pauses can be recorded as ⌴ . Pauses, however, do not usually provide much information, although some children do a lot of figuring out silently, and the pauses can represent a child who otherwise appears not to be using many strategies.

You might find it useful to code teacher assistance besides "try again." For example, for a particular child you might say, "What word would make sense there?" or "Do you know another word that starts that way?" and you may want to devise a code for these kinds of support. However, normally when you take a running record you want to see what the child can do independently, so you will have chosen a book and introduced it so that assistance will not be necessary. The more you intervene, the less reliable your record. In general, it is more helpful to make a record of what the child reads, with you simply noting irregularities or providing additional context to help with later interpretation. For example, I often find it helpful to comment on fluency, pace, any relevant student comments or nervousness, and expression.

Instructionally, the point of running records is to answer these two questions:

- Does the record suggest that the reader is trying to make sense?
- What kind of strategies and sources of information are being used to make meaning?

I also make annotations to record other significant behavior or comments. For example, if a child points to the words for some or all of the text, I would note that. Comments the child makes can also be very revealing about the child's ongoing understanding of the text.

*I*NTERPRETING ORAL READING RECORDS

*T*his part is primarily about the interpretation of the overall running record. It might seem as though this is where the interpretive part begins, but I want to remind you that even when we are making the running record we are necessarily interpreting. We had to decide which behaviors to record (for example, repetitions but not hesitations) and we had to decide whether a reader was self-correcting or just figuring out a word. In this chapter we add a further layer of interpretation as we make sense of our running records (for more on this see Clay 1993a; for an alternative approach see Goodman, Watson, and Burke 1987).

Error Rate

Whatever the recording system used, teachers want to assess how the student is doing. Whether students choose their own books or we choose books for them, we want to make sure they are reading materials they can manage. But what is manageable? The first thing to consider in the running record is the error rate: the proportion of words read incorrectly (although in the long run it is probably more important to ask the students how difficult a book is because doing so gets them to begin thinking about the matter for themselves).

The error rate is simply the ratio of the number of words read incorrectly to the total number of words read. This seems like a reasonable way of estimating how difficult a text is for a child, but it is not perfect for a number of reasons. For many years researchers have argued over which error rate indicates that a text is too difficult ("frustration level"), which indicates that it is very easy ("independent level"), and which indicates that the text is just right. Actually, these arguments are futile, for two reasons. First, all errors are not created equal. Some suggest difficulty with the text whereas others do not. Many substitutions of *a* for *the* and *shouted* for *said* and the like are not the same as substitutions of *jump* for *joker*. Self-corrections may take a lot of mental effort and disrupt reading substantially, or they may not. Hesitations may suggest increased mental effort. Second, some children seem to have a higher tolerance for different kinds of word level errors than do others. Some children's reading processes seem to fall apart when they reach an error rate of about one in twenty (5 percent). Other children seem to feel comfortable, showing healthy reading processes, even in material they read with an error rate of one in eight (12.5 percent). There also appear to be developmental differences in manageable error rate.

Nonetheless, error rate is not a bad indicator of difficulty if we use it cautiously. Marie Clay suggests that an error rate of up to one in twenty (5 percent) indicates that the text is generally easy enough to be read independently. She calls this *easy text*. Text read with an error rate greater than one in ten is considered *hard text*. An error rate of between one in twenty and one in ten is at the edge of what a student can manage without assistance. This is often called *instructional level text,* but let's call it *learning text*. While it provides information that is useful for instruction, it is most important because children actually *learn* from it, provided they are self-correcting appropriately.

In general, running records are of most value when the text is in the learning range because with this kind of text there are not enough errors to disrupt meaning, but it is difficult enough so that many of the strategies used by the reader are overt and able to be recorded.

What Counts as an Error?

Words are easy to count, but errors are less straightforward. Researchers have argued back and forth about what counts as an error, and this is reflected in the various oral reading tests on the market. Table 2 shows the differences between researchers when it comes to counting errors. In a way it depends on what we think we are counting. If we are counting "errors," it hardly seems "fair" to count repetitions, words laboriously figured out, and self-corrections. However, if we are counting "indicators of difficulty," which is, after all, the main reason for counting them at all, it is easier to argue for counting these, and even extensive hesitations. Unfortunately, there is no sensible formula for doing this. There is no way to weight different types of errors. Is an omission as serious as a prolonged hesitation? Is a substitution as serious as an insertion? Is substituting *smell* for *small* the same as substituting *little?*

TABLE 2

Oral Reading Behaviors Counted as "Errors" by Various Authors of Diagnostic Tests

BEHAVIOR	GRAY 1915	GATES 1927	DURRELL 1937	GILMORE 1951	SPACHE 1963	CLAY 1975
Omission of sound and/or word	x	x	x	x	x	x
Addition of sound and/or word	x	x	x	x	x	x
Substitution or mispronunciation	x	x	x	x	x	x
Repetition	x	x	x	x	x	
Self-correction	x		x	x	x	
Word aided	x	x	x	x	x	x
Hesitation		x	x	x		
Punctuation ignored	x		x	x		

Source: From Allington 1984, p. 836. One-word repetitions not counted. The table originally indicated that Clay counted repetitions, which was not accurate. It also indicated as a source Clay 1975. The correct reference is Clay 1972.

I do not see an immediate solution to this, and I don't think one is necessary in most cases. It is probably enough to have a consistent method for counting and a way of making a reasonable explanation when our knowledge tells us that the counting method has failed us in a particular instance. A consistent method of counting allows us to make certain comparisons while being on the lookout for qualitative changes. Since I have used Marie Clay's (1993a) method of recording oral reading behaviors, I also use her method for counting errors, with minor adjustments. Here are the guidelines:

- Omissions count as one error each.
- Insertions count as one error each.
- A word repeatedly read inaccurately counts as an error every time, except when it is a proper noun. Proper nouns count only the first time. For example, if a child continually reads *went* for *want* it counts as an error each time. But if he or she continually reads *Roger* incorrectly, it only counts as an error the first time.
- Words that are pronounced differently because of a child's dialect (for example, *frigeator* for *refrigerator*) do not count as errors.
- Self-corrected words do not count as errors.

- If a page (or two) is omitted, count it as one error but do not count the words in the word count. But if a line is omitted, count each word in that line as an error.
- An intervention in which you tell the child the word counts as one error.
- An intervention with "Try that again" counts as one error. Any other errors in the bracketed section are not counted. Errors made in the second reading of that section are counted. For example, in the following record, the error count is two, one for the TA, and one for the substitution of *a* for *the*. The five errors within the bracketed section do not count.

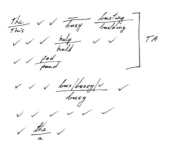

- If there are several ways to record a section, choose the one that fits with your interpretation of the pattern of errors (or the one that fits the child's explanation of it). If that is not possible, choose the one that produces the lowest error count.
- Sometimes you will end up with more errors on a given line than there are words on it, but on any given page, do not count more errors than there are words. Usually in this situation, the reader is creating his or her own text from memory or from the pictures, and there is little point in continuing the running record. Simply note the picture-story match, the quality of the constructed story, and any concepts the child demonstrates about print.

To calculate error rate, divide the number of errors by the number of words in the text, and multiply that figure by 100. For example, if a child makes 15 errors in a 192-word text, the error rate is 15 divided by 192 (which equals about .08) times 100, which equals 8 percent. This can be written as:

$$\text{Error rate} = \frac{\text{Number of errors} \times 100}{\text{Number of words}}$$
$$= \frac{15 \times 100}{192}$$
$$= 8$$

Accuracy is simply this percentage subtracted from 100 percent; in this case it would be 100 percent − 8 percent = 92 percent accuracy.

For practice, calculate the accuracy for the running record of *Busy Beavers* in Tape Example 11 (page 14). The correct calculations are at the bottom of this page.[1]

Self-Correction

At the beginning of the book I explained the importance of self-correction. If children do not correct their own errors, they learn nothing from their mistakes, run the risk of not understanding the text, and may even get to the point of automatically identifying certain words incorrectly. If they do self-correct, there is a good chance that in a literate environment they will teach themselves to read with relatively little help. Thus, it is helpful to have a measurement of how often children correct their own errors. The self-correction rate is the proportion of times a reader corrected her own errors in relation to the number of errors initially made (that is, the number of errors plus the number of self-corrected errors). As a formula, the self-correction rate is the ratio:

Self-corrections : (Errors + Self-corrections)

which is symbolized:

SC : (E + SC)

Calculate the self-correction ratio for the *Busy Beavers* reading (Tape Example 11). The correct calculation is shown at the bottom of this page.[2]

Within the learning range of text difficulty, the self-correction rate can indicate the extent to which readers are monitoring their use of the different sources of information available to them. It is not a perfect indicator, since some readers will monitor their reading and find problems but not correct them overtly. Self-corrections are evidence of the reader comparing different sources of information, finding them discrepant, *and* doing something about correcting the discrepancy. However, as I have mentioned before, some readers go through the process silently.

---

[1]There are 105 words and 1 error, so the error rate is 1 percent:

$$\frac{\text{Errors} \times 100}{\text{Words}} = \frac{1 \times 100}{105} = 1\%$$

The accuracy, then, is 99 percent (100 percent − 1 percent).

[2]There is 1 error (E) and 6 self-corrections (SC) in Tape Example 11.

$$
\begin{aligned}
\text{SC ratio} &= \text{SC} : (\text{E} + \text{SC}) \\
&= 6 : (1 + 6) \\
&= 6 : 7 \\
&= 1 : 7/6 \\
&= 1 : 1.2
\end{aligned}
$$

The self-correction rate, then, is approximately 1 : 1.

Not all self-corrections are equal. It is important to examine which sources of information the reader sees as discrepant. For example, Susan might make substitutions that do not make sense but that would, if written down, look a lot like the word on the page. However, she immediately notices when what she says does not make sense, and she tries again, using both the meaning and the print. We can interpret Susan's running record as suggesting that she is attending most strongly to the print detail but comparing it with a strong internal notion of the meaning of the text. We call this *self-correcting from meaning*. It is as if she says to herself, "That doesn't make sense."

On the other hand, Jane goes about her reading in the opposite manner. She concentrates on meaning, producing substitutions that make sense but that do not fit well with the print. She corrects herself from the print. It is as if she says to herself, "No. That doesn't look right." We call this *self-correcting from print*.

When the text is very easy for readers, they will usually use all the sources of information necessary to get things right the first time. However, as things become harder, they will tend to abandon one or another source of information for a first attempt and then use the neglected source as a check. As things become harder still, they may totally neglect information that they are quite capable of using under normal conditions. Thus, running records taken on material that is too difficult can be quite misleading. They will tell us relatively little of any importance about the reader's strategies, except how they break down.

Prediction

Prediction is at the heart of efficient reading mainly because it is hard to know how to interpret letters or words without knowing the context in which they appear (Bruner 1985). For example, the sound associated with the letter *e* can vary depending on its location in the word, the letters next to it, the letters next-but-one to it, the root of the word, and so forth (consider the sound of *e* in *bed, bead, readmit, give, baker, revere* . . .). In addition, the pronunciation of words depends on their location in the surrounding text. For example, consider the pronunciation of the word *read* in the following contexts:

- I have *Read Along with Mother.*
- I have read that book several times.
- She screamed, "I *have* read along with mother, and I told her she read too fast."

This complexity is partly why predicting is an important aspect of effective reading. Oral reading errors can give some insight into whether or not children are, or are not, predicting. Prediction is an extension of meaning or patterns into the future. Thus, if a reader, without hesitation, makes, or begins to make, a substitution that would make good sense up to that point, but does not fit entirely with the print detail, then he or she is likely to have been predicting. For example, consider the following:

TEXT: One day the teeny tiny woman
       put on her teeny tiny bonnet
READER: One day the teeny tiny woman
        wen—put on her teeny tiny bonnet

In this case the reader predicted that the word *went* would begin the next line, but got there and did not find the letters expected. There might be other explanations for this reading, but prediction fits best with our own experience: as mature readers, we do it all the time.

The next two examples on the tape illustrate prediction. They do not require any new recording techniques.

TAPE EXAMPLE 15: *Indian Two Feet and His Horse* by Margaret Friskey (1959)

There was
a little Indian.
He wished
he had a horse.

The running record should look like this:

TAPE EXAMPLE 16: *Saturday Morning* by Lesley Moyes (1983)

Mum hosed the garden.
"Please will you hose me?"
said Helen.
"Please will you hose me?"
said Mark.
Mum hosed Helen and Mark.

The running record is the following:

In the first example, Emily predicted that the story would begin "There once was . . ." but she looked and either saw some letters there that disagreed (*once* does start with the same sound as *was,* but *was* does not have an *n*), or she went on to the next line and saw *a* and realized that you can't say "There once a," so she corrected herself.

In the second example, we heard Nick predicting on two levels. Using normal conversation, Mark *asks* a question, so the text should say, "asked Mark," but it doesn't, so Nick corrected himself. Then, when he got to the bottom of the page, he began to predict where the story would go next, and looked for verification when he turned the page. In contrast to this is the child who substitutes nonsense words or words that do not fit the context. It is unlikely that such a reader is predicting.

It is always helpful to have several examples of a particular type of error in order to be comfortable with what you are inferring. However, sometimes you see a single example of an error that is almost certainly a result of prediction and you can say with reasonable certainty that the student does predict while reading. Although we all spend our lives predicting what will be said next when we converse with others, what will happen in traffic when we are driving, and so forth, it is still important to be able to say that a child predicts when reading because it means that the child understands at some level that the point of reading is to make sense.

Prediction produces words that make sense up to that point, although they do not necessarily fit the letters that are on the page or the words that follow. In other words, substitutions that make sense in context often suggest that the child has predicted. However, there are exceptions. For example, if a reader comes to a word with which he has difficulty, pauses, and then says a word that makes sense up to that point and fits with some of the print detail, it is evidence that he is trying to make sense and to integrate cues, but not that he is predicting. Prediction takes place *before* you get there, not after.

The Balance and Method of Information Use

When I study children's oral reading, I am most interested in the information they use and how they use it. In a book that is not too easy and not too hard for them,

I want to know whether they use the available information from their language, from their experience, and from the page in a flexible and active manner. I want to know whether they try to stay a little ahead of what they are reading, and whether they check one source of information against another. Sometimes problems occur. For example, some children rely on one source of information to the exclusion of another. They may rely on their knowledge of the alphabetic system, for example, without checking against their knowledge of the language or their own experience. An oral reading such as the following might occur:

TEXT: I cannot go out to play with you today.

READER: I cannot go oot to play with you todda.

There are, of course, a number of possible reasons for this kind of pattern. The readers might not have the relevant experience, or their language pattern may be substantially different from that of the text, or they may not have learned "book language." They may have come to doubt the relevance or adequacy of their own knowledge or language. Their interpretation of reading instruction might have convinced them that reading has nothing to do with making sense. Whatever the cause, we should try to encourage these readers to make more use of these other sources of information in conjunction with what they already use. At the same time, we will certainly be interested in seeing whether something in the classroom (or at home) is contributing to the problem. For example, if the books such readers have in class are too difficult, their error rate may make it impossible for them to construct meaning from the text. Consistently deprived of meaningfulness in activities designated as reading, they may have developed unfortunate reading habits and misconceptions about reading itself.

Similarly, we may see imbalances in the use of information sources in the opposite direction. Some children depend too heavily on their own knowledge and language patterns, and more or less ignore what is on the page. For example:

TEXT: Down came the biscuits
             and the book
             and the bucket

READER: Down came cookies
             down came the pails
             down came the books

It is true that readers must construct meaning using their own knowledge. Some reading situations (such as reading a paperback novel) do not require much concern over the use of exactly those words the author used. However, other types of reading (such as instructions for running expensive or dangerous machines) require detailed attention to the words the author used. Good readers are flexible in their use of the different sources of information, and we teachers should encourage readers who ignore too much of what is on the page to attend more to print detail, particularly when checking predictions. Such readers usually are predicting, but they do not verify their predictions. They may lack the knowledge of print conventions or of alphabetic relationships, or they may have such knowledge but fail to use it.

It is very common for children to pay too much attention to one cue source or another for brief periods of time and in particular situations (Biemiller 1970, 1979); and it is quite common for children who are just getting the hang of letter-sound relationships to devote too much effort to them, even to the extent that they lose meaning as they read. Rereading at such times can substantially improve performance. Similarly, children who overpredict will perform better when asked to follow the text with a finger.

Although readers should show a balanced use of sources of information, they should also use the information flexibly and strategically in the service of meaning. If one strategy fails, are other strategies used? Are the strategies efficient? These are important questions to ask of running records. For example, we might see children rereading sentences, parts of sentences, or paragraphs. This can be an effective strategy, but if it is used as the major method for figuring out unfamiliar words, it is inefficient. We might observe children repeatedly rereading parts of a sentence to help figure out a word in a situation where rereading from the beginning of the sentence would give better contextual support. Sometimes we see readers who simply give up after one attempt at each problematic word. There are no hard and fast guidelines as to what constitutes efficient reading strategies, except to say that flexible use of strategies and information sources is likely to be most efficient, provided that readers clearly direct their efforts toward the goal of constructing meaning.

Analyzing running records this way leads us to examine each deviation from the print to see what type of cues readers have used: *meaning* (M), *structure* (S), or *visual* (V) cues. We can then make a record of the analysis down the side of the page.

Here is an example:

TEXT:	Danny ran to his house
	and went to his room.
READER:	Danny ran to his hus
	and ran to his room.

The completed running record would look like this:

NAME:					DATE:			E	SC	E	SC
BOOK:										MSV	MSV
✓	✓	✓	✓	$\frac{hus}{house}$				/		✓	
✓	$\frac{ran}{went}$	✓	✓	✓				/		ms	

Analyzing running records in this way allows us to check our intuition about the reader's use of the available cues and later to see at a glance changes in these patterns.

Cues can be used both to identify a word and to correct an error. For example, a reader can predict (M and possibly S) and then self-correct from print (V). This is different from first trying the word from visual cues (V), then self-correcting because it doesn't make sense (M) or because it doesn't sound right (S).

One way to simplify the recording is to print running record sheets that have columns down the right-hand side specifically for analysis, as shown in the example above and in the remainder of the examples in this chapter (a blank form is provided in Appendix A). One column can be made for the analysis of errors (E) and one for analysis of self-corrections (SC). You might also have a column for tallying the number of errors and another column for self-corrections, as in the form in Appendix A.

Since the letters M, S, V are always written in the same order, we can simply write

M S V
M V
S V

and so forth for each error or self-correction. The absence of an M in the third sequence above shows the failure to use meaning as a cue. Thus,

TEXT: He went down the street
READER: He went down the road—street

would be recorded as follows:

NAME:	DATE:			E	SC	E	SC
BOOK:						MSV	MSV
✓ ✓ ✓ ✓	$\frac{read}{street}$ /sc					/	ms	✓

Alternatively, you may write MSV for every line and circle the cues that were used.

The MSV analysis is not as simple as it might appear. You will certainly encounter differences of opinion over whether particular cues were used. For instance, if the text word has only two out of eight letters in common with the word the child said, does that count as use of visual cues? What about two out of four? You must use your judgment on such matters, keeping in mind that ultimately it is the *pattern* you should be concerned about, not each individual error. You will not be able to say for sure that a reader used a particular cue system. All you can do is say that what the reader did was or was not consistent with some cue systems and that your hypothesis fits the data. For example, suppose a child reads as follows:

TEXT: Once there were
READER: Once upon—once there were

One possible cause of this self-correction is that the child predicted "upon" but when his eyes got to the word he noticed that the wrong letters were there (visual cues), so he corrected himself. Another possibility is that he predicted "upon" with such confidence that he paid little attention to the letters there and proceeded to the next word, "were," which he recognized. Realizing that "Once upon were" doesn't sound right (structure cues), he corrected himself. We can ask the child how he managed to correct himself, but we will never know for sure. In short, do not get caught up too much worrying over individual examples unless there are larger disagreements over patterns.

All Together Now

To pull it all together, try taking a running record of *Owl Babies*, an excellent children's book. It is the last example on side A of the tape.

TAPE EXAMPLE 17: *Owl Babies* by Martin Waddell; illustrated by
Patrick Benson (1992)

Once there were three baby owls:
Sarah and Percy and Bill.

They lived in a hole
in the trunk of a tree
with their Owl Mother.
The hole had twigs and
leaves and owl feathers in it.
It was their house.

One night they woke up and
their Owl Mother was GONE.
"Where's mommy?" asked Sarah.
"Oh my goodness!" said Percy.
"I want my mommy!" said Bill.

The baby owls *thought*
(all owls think a lot)—
"I think she's gone hunting," said Sarah.
"To get us our food!" said Percy.
"I want my mommy!" said Bill.

But their Owl Mother didn't come.
The baby owls came out of
their house, and they sat
on the tree and waited.

A big branch for Sarah,
a small branch for Percy,
and an old piece of ivy for Bill.
"She'll be back," said Sarah.
"Back *soon!*" said Percy.
"I want my mommy!" said Bill.

It was dark in the woods and
they had to be brave, for things
moved all around them.
"She'll bring us mice and
things that are nice," said Sarah.
"I suppose so!" said Percy.
"I want my mommy!" said Bill.

They sat and they thought
(all owls think a lot)—
"I think we should *all*
sit on *my* branch," said Sarah.
And they did, all three together.

"Suppose she got lost," said Sarah.
"Or a fox got her!" said Percy.
"I want my mommy!" said Bill.
And the baby owls closed
their owl eyes and wished their
Owl Mother would come.

AND SHE CAME.

Soft and silent, she swooped
through the trees
to Sarah and Percy
and Bill.

"Mommy!" they cried,
and they flapped and they danced,
and they bounced up and down
on their branch.

"WHAT'S ALL THE FUSS?"
their Owl Mother asked.
"You knew I'd come back."
The baby owls thought
(all owls think a lot)—
"I knew it," said Sarah.
"And I knew it!" said Percy.
"I love my mommy!" said Bill.

The analyzed running record can be found on pages 35–38. Notice the consistent pattern of cues used in the reading. For Sam, words had to make sense and sound right first. They also had to look right, but that was a secondary concern (by a small margin).

Educators may want to ask, "Did she comprehend what she read?" I think we could easily answer in the affirmative just from listening to the expressiveness in Sam's voice. Better questions might be "Is Sam reading to make sense?" and "What sort of engagement did Sam have with this text?" To answer the first of these two questions, aside from her expression, Sam's use of cues reveals an emphasis on meaning, as does her use of strategies. Viewing her reading this way makes it unnecessary for us to examine it on every occasion, as her focus on meaning and her strategic efforts in the service of meaning suggest that Sam understands that meaning is what reading is about. She is unlikely to change her mind on her next reading. The answer to the second question—what sort of engagement Sam had with the text—draws our attention to other features, such as her persistence in

NAME: Sam J.	DATE: 1/24/96	E	SC	E	SC
BOOK: Owl Babies	P.①			MSV	MSV

				E	SC	E MSV	SC MSV
✓ ✓ <u>was</u> <u>were</u> ✓ ✓ <u>ow/R/✓</u> owls				1		m s ✓	
✓ ✓ ✓ ✓ ✓							
✓ ✓ ✓ ✓ ✓							
✓ ✓ ✓ ✓ ✓ ✓							
✓ R² ✓ ✓ ✓							
✓ ✓ ✓ <u>twig/tig/trig/t/tig/✓</u> ✓ Twigs							
<u>l/✓</u> ✓ ✓ ✓ ✓ ✓ leaves							
✓ ✓ ✓ <u>ho me</u> house				1		m s ✓	
✓ ✓ ✓ ✓ ✓ ✓							
✓ ✓ ✓ ✓ ✓							
✓ <u>m/✓/mom/sc</u> <u>s/sc</u> ✓ mom my asked				1 1		m s ✓ m s	✓ ✓
<u>w/wha/how/sc</u> ✓ <u>gad/R</u> ✓ ✓ oh goodness T				1		m s ✓ ms ✓	ms
✓ ✓ ✓ ✓ ✓ ✓							
<u>They/sc</u> <u>babies/sc</u> <u>ow/R/✓</u> ✓ The baby owls				1 1		m s ✓ m s ✓ ms	✓ ms
✓ ✓ ✓ ✓				1		m s ✓	
✓ ✓ <u>the</u> <u>got/R/goed/sc/R</u> ✓ ✓ ✓ she's gone				1		m s ✓	✓
✓ ✓ ✓ <u>w/✓</u> ✓ ✓ ✓ our							
✓ ✓ ✓ ✓ ✓ ✓				④	⑥		

Words (W) =   Error Rate (ER) = E/W x 100 =
Self-corrections (SC) = Accuracy = 100 - ER =
Errors (E) =   Self-correction rate = SC : SC + E =

figuring out words and in reading a lengthy text, and particularly her commentary along the way. Her comments suggest not merely that she understood, but the ways in which she understood—the qualities of her engagement. The following are her comments while she read, and what they suggest to me:

SAM: "Twigs" is a hard word. [She reflects on the process and estimates difficulty. I could have asked her what made it hard which might have led to some focused and timely instruction].

SAM: They just said that they lived in it up here. Why do they say it again? [Critical reading of author's style.]

NAME: SAM J.	DATE: 1/24/94	E	SC	E	SC
BOOK: Owl Babies continued P.2				MSV	MSV

✓ ✓ ✓ ✓ ✓ ✓
✓ babies/baby ✓ ✓ ✓ ✓ | 1 | msv ✓
✓ ✓ ✓ w/R/w/R/sc ✓ | 1 | ms | ✓
✓ their/sc They ✓ ✓ watched/waited | 1 | msv | ✓
✓ the/ ✓   1 | | msv

✓ ✓ ✓ ✓ ✓
✓ ✓ ✓ ✓ ✓
✓ ✓ ✓ ✓ ✓ ✓ ✓
she/she'll /sc ✓ soon/said /sc /R² ✓ | 1 | msv | ✓
  | 1 | msv | ✓
✓ ✓ ✓ ✓
✓ ✓ ✓ ✓ ✓ ✓

✓ ✓ ✓ ✓ ✓ fores/woods /R /sc ✓ | 1 | ms | ✓
✓ ✓ ✓ ✓ ✓ ✓
✓ ✓ ✓ ✓
✓ he/bring /sc ✓R ✓ ✓ | 1 | msv | ✓
✓ ✓ ✓ ✓ ✓ ✓
✓ ✓ ✓ s/said /R/✓/R sarah/Percy /R /sc | 1 | ms | ✓
✓ ✓ ✓ ✓ ✓ ✓

①②

Words (W) =
Self-corrections (SC) =
Errors (E) =

Error Rate (ER) = E/W x 100 =
Accuracy = 100 - ER =
Self-correction rate = SC : SC + E =

SAM: I feel sad for Bill. He must miss his Mommy a lot. [Connection to own experience and empathy for character.]

SAM: These are good pictures! Look at the leaves and the branches. See the little lines? Isn't that good? . . . And isn't it good that he did, like, blue on the sides? . . . I can't even do those black lines on there. [Appreciation for the craft of the illustrator in the use of detail and color. She is also viewing herself as a possible illustrator but one who currently lacks the particular skills possessed by the book illustrator.]

SAM: He might think he messed . . . Who's this from again? . . . Is that a boy

NAME: Sam J.	DATE: 1/24/94	E	SC	E	SC
BOOK: Owl Babies continued P. 3				MSV	MSV

The | sc ✓ ✓ thought | R | sc ✓ | | 1 | ms v | ✓
They   they | | 1 | ms v | ✓
✓ ✓ ✓ ✓
✓ ✓ | thin | v | R ✓ ✓ ✓
       think
✓ ✓ ✓ ✓ ✓ ✓
✓ ✓ ✓ ✓ ✓ to | ✓
                    together

s s s | soup | os ✓ ✓ ✓ ✓ ✓ | | 1 | | ✓
suppose | T
✓ ✓ ✓ ✓ ✓ ✓ ✓
✓ ✓ ✓ ✓ ✓ ✓
✓ ✓ ✓ ✓ ✓
✓ ✓ ✓ ✓ ✓ ✓
✓ ✓ will | came | sc | | 1 | | m s v
       would   come | | 1 | | m v | sv
✓ ✓ ✓

Softly | sc ✓ R ✓ ✓ ✓ | | 1 | m s v | ✓
Soft
ther | R | the | R | sc ✓ ✓ | | 1 | m s v | ✓
Through
✓ ✓ ✓ ✓
✓ ✓

(2) (5)

Words (W) =   Error Rate (ER) = E/W x 100 =
Self-corrections (SC) =   Accuracy = 100 - ER =
Errors (E) =   Self-correction rate = SC : SC + E =

or a girl? . . . He thinks he messed up, but it really looks good. Or maybe he thought that it looked good, but then first he thought that it looked bad and then he said, "Oh, I think it looks good." [Awareness of authorship—in this case that of the illustrator—and that authors are ordinary people who have feelings and evaluate their own work.]

SAM: Wait a minute, Dad! There's a problem. How can Bill get down to his Ivy? Baby owls can't fly.

ME: Maybe they hop.

NAME: Sam J.		DATE: 1/24/94	E	SC	E	SC
BOOK: Owl Babies		continued P.4			MSV	MSV

```
✓  ✓   all/R/sc   ✓
            ‾
I/sc   ✓/R/th/R/✓   ✓ ✓ ✓ ✓  ⌉ TA        1
and        they                ⌉
–  –  –   –   –   –             ⌋
✓   ✓   ✓
✓   ✓   ✓
✓   ✓   ✓   ✓ ✓   p/b/App/da/dankd/✓
                        danced
✓  ✓  jumped  ✓  ✓  ✓                       1          ms
        bounced
✓   ✓   ✓
_____
✓   ✓   ✓   ✓
✓   ✓   ✓   cried                           1          ms
                asked
✓   ✓   ✓   ✓  ✓
✓   ✓   ✓   ✓
✓   ✓   ✓   ✓   ✓
✓   ✓   ✓   ✓   ✓
I/sc   n/R/sc   ✓  ✓  ✓  ✓              1   ms   ✓
and      I
✓  ✓  ✓  ✓  ✓  ✓                        1   ms   ✓
                                      ③  ②
```

Words (W) = 323   Error Rate (ER) = E/W x 100 = 3%
Self-corrections (SC) = 21   Accuracy = 100 - ER = 97%
Errors (E) = 10   Self-correction rate = SC : SC + E = 2:3
                                     = 1:1.5

SAM: How can they hop? They would be scared . . . [Goes on to discuss how it would be possible to get from one point to another on the tree.] [This is a critical reading of the logic of the story as portrayed in the text and illustrations. Her analysis includes the physical probability and the emotional probability, and the consideration of alternative possibilities.]

SAM: I like how he said that. [Appreciation for author style and character development.]

SAM: Sarah always says stuff like that. [Reflecting, accurately or not, on character development.]

SAM: They'll do it one more time and that'll be three times they say that. In one of the first parts they said it, and they said it right here, and they're going to say it at the end. [Analyzing structure of the text.]

SAM: [Can't figure it out.] And that one doesn't give you any pictures. [Considering strategy options.]

SAM: She has pretty eyes.

SAM: I like Bill. Bill's plump. Plump. And Sarah is big. She's a big owl. I think that's Sarah. [Connecting text image to illustration.]

SAM: Is that a *B* or a *D*? [Awareness of the source of a problem.]

SAM: I didn't read that one . . . I just goed straight to "on their branch." [Analyzing her own error.]

Sam's comments help us to understand her understanding. If you want children to have such conversations, remember that they are most common:

- After multiple readings.
- In contexts that maintain reading as a social activity.
- When the texts being read are engaging, manageable, and relevant.
- When other people they know engage in commenting on what they read.

It shouldn't be too difficult to remember these conditions if you consider your own experiences as a reader.

Some Caveats

Running records are not perfect reflections of children's oral reading, let alone perfect reflections of their reading in general. However, they do provide some extremely useful data that can both document change and direct instruction. They provide indirect evidence of how children are going about understanding what they are reading. A number of studies have shown that particular patterns of errors are strongly related to other measures of understanding: cloze tests and retellings, both of which will be discussed in later chapters. Increases in self-correction alone, given a comparable error rate, suggest a greater degree of understanding. However, more consistent indicators of competence can be produced by adding together different oral reading behaviors (Sadoski and Lee 1986). In general, it is unnecessary to engage in mathematical exercises to show change, but studies do show a strong relationship between healthy patterns of oral reading behavior and other indicators of healthy reading.

When talking about change over time we can look at changes in readers' cue use and integration, range and flexibility of strategy use, persistence, fluency, book difficulty, expression, and confidence. Some of these are not recorded in the running record per se, but can be important annotations on the record. For example, fluency can range from fluent to finger-pointing (when children point with their finger at each word as they read) to voice-pointing (when children do not use their finger, but separate each word orally as if they were using their finger). Expression is also an area to consider, and is an indicator of the sense that the reader is making, as are comments made during and after the reading. Annotations describing the context are also important, both for understanding the particular reading and for comparing records over time. For example, a tenth reading is not the same as a first exposure to a book.

Running records have some bonuses. In my experience, when I begin to take running records, students generally want to know what I am doing. I explain what I am doing and that I will show them the record and explain it when they have finished reading. Students find this interesting, and it gets them thinking about their reading through the records. Also, it is easy with running records to highlight the positive. To begin with, you have a page of check marks with only a few other marks, with the check marks visual evidence of all the words the student read correctly. You can also highlight the value of the strategies the student used. Sharing the records with the student is important. Sometimes it leads them to record each other's reading, which provokes further discussion of the process.

When you are beginning to learn how to take and analyze running records, you will need to skip sections occasionally when you fall behind the reader. Just draw a double line and pick up again on the next page or paragraph. But every now and then it is O.K. to ask a student to stop for a moment while you catch up because you are just learning and she is reading so fast. This is good news for less competent readers—they are doing well and you are a novice. Very good for the confidence, this!

Some students in the beginning may be a bit anxious about the records, especially if they can hear you taking them. For example, if you use a pencil on a piece of paper on a wooden desk, it is often quite easy to hear the difference between a check mark and some other record. If a student is nervous and starts focusing on the sounds of your record rather than her inner monitor, self-monitoring goes out the window, replaced by the monitoring of your pencil. A student who is thus concerned can be helped if you discuss the records and share them, but you may also reduce the problem simply by substituting a ball-point pen on a pad of paper for the pencil and single sheet. Also, if you are right-handed, try to sit on the right-hand side of the student; otherwise the recording paper will be too close to the student and you may find yourself poking her in the eye with your elbow.

Remember, Appendix B contains further practice examples of running records to help you become more automatic in your recording.

A P P E N D I X A

NAME:	DATE:	E	SC	E	SC
BOOK:				MSV	MSV

Words (W) =
Self-corrections (SC) =
Errors (E) =

Error Rate (ER) = E/W x 100 =
Accuracy = 100 - ER =
Self-correction rate = SC : SC + E =

APPENDIX B

Practice Running Records

Here are examples of running records that appear on side B of the audiotape accompanying this book.

TAPE EXAMPLE 18: *Oops!* by Fran Hunia (1984)

(The completed running records are on pages 46–47.)

Page 4:
Billy wanted a biscuit . . .

Page 5:
but
he
couldn't
reach.

Page 6:
He stood on a chair . . .

Page 7:
but
he
couldn't
reach.

Page 8:
He put a box
on the chair . . .

Page 9:
but
he
couldn't
reach.

Page 10:
He put a bucket
on the box
on the chair . . .

Page 11:
but
he
couldn't
reach.

Page 12:
He put a book
on the bucket
on the box
on the chair
but

Page 13:
OOPS!

Page 14:
Down came the biscuits
and the book
and the bucket
and the box
and the chair . . .

Page 15:
and Billy.

Page 16:
Silly Billy!

TAPE EXAMPLE 19:   *Greedy Cat* by Joy Cowley (1983b)

(The completed running records are on pages 48–49.)
Page 3:
Mum went shopping
and got some sausages.
Along came Greedy Cat.
He looked in the shopping bag.
Gobble, gobble, gobble,
and that was the end of that.

Page 5:
Mum went shopping
and got some sticky buns.

Along came Greedy Cat.
He looked in the shopping bag.
Gobble, gobble, gobble,
and that was the end of that.

Page 7:
Mum went shopping
and got some potato chips.
Along came Greedy Cat.
He looked in the shopping bag.
Gobble, gobble, gobble,
and that was the end of that.

Page 8:
Mum went shopping
and got some bananas.

Page 9:
Along came Greedy Cat.
He looked in the shopping bag.
Gobble, gobble, gobble,
and that was the end of that.

Page 10:
Mum went shopping
and got some chocolate.

Page 11:
Along came Greedy Cat.
He looked in the shopping bag.
Gobble, gobble, gobble,
and that was the end of that.

Page 13:
Mum went shopping
and got a pot of pepper.

Page 14:
Along came Greedy Cat.
He looked in the shopping bag.
Gobble, gobble—

Page 15:
YOW!

Page 16:
and that was the end of that!

TAPE EXAMPLE 20:   *The Terrible Days of My Cat Cali* by William Haggerty
(1990)

(The completed running record is on page 50.)
Once my cat bit me on the nose when I was
asleep. And once she came back on Friday
and did nothing, just sit down in some shed.
Then she came home.

Page 2:
Once my cat climbed on the screen. After my
cat climbed on the screen, she went upstairs
and got under the covers in my mother's bed
and slept for one hour.

Page 3:
After she came out of the covers, she ran
downstairs and purred at the basement door.
Instead of going in the basement door, she
cried at the front door and ran around the
house two times. Then she chased after a
motorcycle. She came back home and she was
hungry.

Page 4:
And today she ran away, but my brother found
her. She made us late for Reading!

NAME: *Amanda*	①	DATE: *9 / 12 / 96*	E	SC	E MSV	SC MSV
BOOK: *Oops!*						

✓ ✓ ✓ ✓ ____

5. ✓
✓
✓
✓ ____

6. ✓ ✓ ✓ ✓ ✓ ____

7. ✓
✓
✓
✓
✓ ____

8. ✓ | $\frac{st}{put}$ | $\frac{sc}{\ }$ ✓ ✓ | 1 | ms | ✓
✓ ✓ ✓ ____

9. ✓
✓
✓
✓ ____

10. ✓ ✓ ✓ $\frac{box}{bucket}$ | 1 | msv
✓ ✓ ✓
✓ ✓ ✓

Words (W) =
Self-corrections (SC) =
Errors (E) =

Error Rate (ER) = E/W x 100 =
Accuracy = 100 - ER =
Self-correction rate = SC : SC + E =

Running record for Oops! *by Fran Hunia*

NAME: *Amanda* ② DATE: 9/12/96	E	SC	E MSV	SC MSV
BOOK: *Oops!*				

```
11.
   ✓
   ✓
   ✓
   ✓
   ─────────────────
12.
   ✓  ✓  ✓  box                                    1        m s ✓
            book
   ✓ ✓R ✓
   an /sc  ✓ ✓                                          1    m s      ✓
   on
   ✓  ✓  ✓
   ✓
   ─────────────────
13.
   ✓
   ─────────────────
14.
   ✓  ✓  ✓  ✓
   ✓  ✓  ✓
   ✓ ✓ pa /sc                                        1        m s      ✓
        bucket
   ✓  ✓  ✓
   ✓  ✓  ✓
   ─────────────────
15.
   on /on /sc  ✓                                         1    m s      ✓
   and
   ─────────────────
16.
   ✓  ✓
```

	E	SC
	2	4

Words (W) = 77
Self-corrections (SC) = 4
Errors (E) = 2

Error Rate (ER) = E/W x 100 = 2/77 × 100 = 3
Accuracy = 100 - ER = 97%
Self-correction rate = SC : SC + E = 4:6
= 1:1.5

Running record for Oops! (continued)

		E	SC	E MSV	SC MSV
BOOK: Greedy Cat					

```
3.  ✓  ✓  ✓
    ✓  ✓  ✓  ✓
    ✓  ✓  ✓  ✓
    ✓  ✓  ✓  ✓   ‾‾‾‾‾‾    ✓                    |              |
                 shopping
    and   he    ‾‾‾‾‾                            |       m s
    ‾‾‾   ‾‾‾   gobble|T   ✓   ✓                 |       m s
    ✓  ✓  ✓  ✓  ✓  ✓  ✓                          |       ‾

5.  momma   ✓   ✓                                |       m s V
    Mum
    ✓  ✓  ✓  ✓  biscuits                         |       m s V
                 buns
    ✓ R  ✓  ✓  ✓
    ✓  ✓  ✓  ✓  ‾‾‾‾‾‾‾   ✓                       |
                 shopping
    ✓  ✓  ✓
    ✓  ✓  ✓  ✓  ✓  ✓  ✓

7.  Momma   ✓   ✓                                |       m s V
    Mum
    ✓  ‾‾‾  ‾‾‾  ‾‾‾  ‾‾‾                         |
       got  some  potato  chips                  |
                                                 |
                                                 |
    al/ ✓  ‾‾‾  ✓  ✓  ✓                          |
    along
    ✓  ✓  ✓  ✓  ‾‾‾‾‾‾                           |       m s
                 shopping
    ✓  ✓  ✓
    ✓  ✓  ✓  ✓  ✓  ✓  ✓
```

Words (W) =   Error Rate (ER) = E/W x 100 =
Self-corrections (SC) =   Accuracy = 100 - ER =
Errors (E) =   Self-correction rate = SC : SC + E =

Running record for Greedy Cat *by Joy Cowley*

	E	SC	E MSV	SC MSV
8. Momma ✓ ✓ Mum ✓ ✓ ✓ ✓	1		MSV	
9. and/al/sc ✓ ✓ ✓ along ✓ ✓ ✓ ✓ s̄hopping ✓ ✓ ✓ ✓ ✓ ✓ ✓ ✓ ✓ ✓		1 1	ms ms	V
10. ✓ ✓ ✓ ✓ ✓ ✓ ✓				
11. ✓ ✓ ✓ ✓ and ✓ ✓ ✓ s̄hopping ✓ he ✓ ✓ ✓ ✓ ✓ ✓ ✓ ✓ ✓✓	1 1		ms	
13. Momma ✓ ✓ Mum ✓ ✓ ✓ ✓	1		msV	
14. ✓ ✓ ✓ ✓ ✓ ✓ ✓ s̄hopping ✓	1			
15. on y̱ou	1		msV	
16. ✓ ✓ ✓ ✓ ✓ ✓ ✓	20	1		

Words (W) = 166
Self-corrections (SC) = 1
Errors (E) = 20

Error Rate (ER) = E/W x 100 = 20/166 × 100 = 12
Accuracy = 100 - ER = 88%
Self-correction rate = SC : SC + E = 1:21

Running record for Greedy Cat *(continued)*

NAME: Billy			DATE: 6/6/96		E	SC	E	SC
BOOK: My Cat Cali							MSV	MSV

1. ✓ ✓ ✓ ✓ ✓ ✓ ✓ ✓ ✓ ✓
✓ ✓ ✓ ✓ ✓ ✓ ✓ ✓
✓ ✓ ✓ ✓ ✓ ✓ and/sc ✓ ✓ ___ 1 | ms | | V
                    in
✓ ✓ ✓ ✓
_____

2. ✓ ✓ ✓ ✓ ✓ ✓ ✓ ✓ ✓
✓ ✓ ✓ ✓ ✓ ✓ ✓ ✓
✓ ✓ ✓ ✓ ✓ ✓ ✓ ✓ ✓R
✓ ✓ ✓ ✓ ✓
_____

3. ✓ ✓ ✓ ✓ ✓ ✓ ✓ ✓
✓ ✓ ✓ ✓ ✓ ✓ ✓
and/R²/sc ✓ ✓ ✓ ✓ ✓ ✓   1 | ms | | V
instead
✓ ✓ ✓ ✓ ✓ ✓ ✓ ✓
✓ ✓ ✓ and/the/sc ✓ do/sc ✓ ✓   1 | ms | | V
        then   chased   1 | ms | | V
✓ ✓ ✓ ✓ ✓ ✓
✓
_____

4. ✓ ✓ ✓ ✓ ✓ ✓ cat/R ✓
✓R sh/✓ ✓ ✓ ✓ ✓
   she

Words (W) = 129
Self-corrections (SC) = 4
Errors (E) = 0

Error Rate (ER) = E/W x 100 = 0
Accuracy = 100 - ER = 100%
Self-correction rate = SC : SC + E = 4 : 4
                                     1 : 1

Running record for The Terrible Days of My Cat Cali *by William Haggerty*

EFERENCES

Children's Books

Brownell, M. Barbara. 1988. *Busy Beavers*. Washington, DC: National Geographic Society.

Cowley, Joy. 1983a. *Going to School*. Auckland, New Zealand: Shortland.

———. 1983b. *Greedy Cat*. Wellington, New Zealand: Learning Media Limited.

———. 1984. *Old Tuatara*. Wellington, New Zealand: Department of Education.

Friskey, Margaret. 1959. *Indian Two Feet and His Horse*. Illustrated by Katherine Evans. Chicago: Children's Press.

Haggerty, William. 1990. *The Terrible Days of My Cat Cali*. Self-published.

Hunia, Fran. 1984. *Oops!* Auckland, New Zealand: Ashton Scholastic.

Mahy, Margaret. 1984a. *The Dragon's Birthday*. Illustrated by Philip Webb. Auckland, New Zealand: Shortland Educational Publications.

———. 1984b. *Fantail, Fantail*. Illustrated by Bruce Phillips. Wellington, New Zealand: Department of Education.

Malcolm, Margaret. 1983. *I Can Read*. Wellington, New Zealand: Department of Education.

Martin, Craig. 1982. *My Bike*. Wellington, New Zealand: Department of Education. (Distributed in the United States by Richard C. Owen.)

Mayer, Mercer. 1968. *There's a Nightmare in My Closet*. New York: E. P. Dutton.

Melser, June. 1981. *Little Pig*. Illustrated by Isabel Lowe. San Diego: The Wright Group.

Moyes, Lesley. 1983. *Saturday Morning*. Wellington, New Zealand: Department of Education.

Nodset, Joan. 1989. *Who Took the Farmer's Hat?* Illustrated by Fritz Siebel. Lexington, MA: D.C. Heath and Co.

Waddell, Martin. 1992. *Owl Babies*. Cambridge, MA: Candlewick Press.

Ziefert, Harriet. 1989. *Harry Goes to Funland*. Illustrated by Mavis Smith. New York: Penguin Putnam.

Professional Resources

Allington, Richard. 1983. The Reading Instruction Provided Readers of Differing Reading Abilities. *Elementary School Journal* 83: 255–265.

————. 1984. Oral Reading. In P. David Pearson, ed., *Handbook of Reading Research*, pp. 829–864. White Plains, NY: Longman.

Biemiller, Andrew. 1970. The Development of the Use of Graphic and Contextual Information as Children Learn to Read. *Reading Research Quarterly* 6: 75–96.

————. 1979. Changes in the Use of Graphic and Contextual Information as Functions of Passage Difficulty and Reading Achievement Level. *Journal of Reading Behavior* 11: 308–318.

Bruner, Jerome. 1985. Models of the Learner. *Educational Researcher* 14, 6: 5–8.

Clay, Marie M. 1966. Emergent Reading Behavior. Ph.D. diss. University of Auckland, New Zealand.

————. 1972. *The Early Detection of Reading Difficulties: A Diagnostic Survey.* Auckland, New Zealand: Heinemann.

————. 1975. *What Did I Write?* Portsmouth, NH: Heinemann.

————. 1991. *Becoming Literate: The Construction of Inner Control.* Portsmouth, NH: Heinemann.

————. 1993a. *An Observation Survey of Early Literacy Achievement.* Portsmouth, NH: Heinemann.

————. 1993b. *Reading Recovery: A Guidebook for Teachers in Training.* Portsmouth, NH: Heinemann.

Goodman, Kenneth. 1965. A Linguistic Study of Cues and Miscues in Reading. *Elementary English* 42: 639–643.

Goodman, Kenneth, Dorothy Watson, and Carolyn Burke. 1987. *Reading Miscue Analysis.* New York: Richard C. Owen.

Johnston, Peter H. 1997. *Knowing Literacy: Constructive Literacy Assessment.* York, ME: Stenhouse.

Leu, Don. 1982. Oral Reading Error Analysis: A Critical Review of Research and Application. *Reading Research Quarterly* 17: 420-437.

New Zealand Department of Education. 1980. Early Reading Inservice Course. Wellington: P.D. Hasselberg Government Printer.

Sadoski, Mark, and Sharon Lee. 1986. Reading Comprehension and Miscue Combination Scores: Further Analysis and Comparison. *Reading Research and Instruction* 25: 160–167.

Schumm, Jeanne, and R. Scott Baldwin. 1989. Cue System Usage in Oral and Silent Reading. *Journal of Reading Behavior* 21, (2): 141–154.

Weber, Rose Marie. 1970. A Linguistic Analysis of First-Grade Reading Errors. *Reading Research Quarterly* 5: 427–451.